PIXAR

THE ULTIMATE COLLECTION

MONSTERS, INC. AND MONSTERS UNIVERSITY

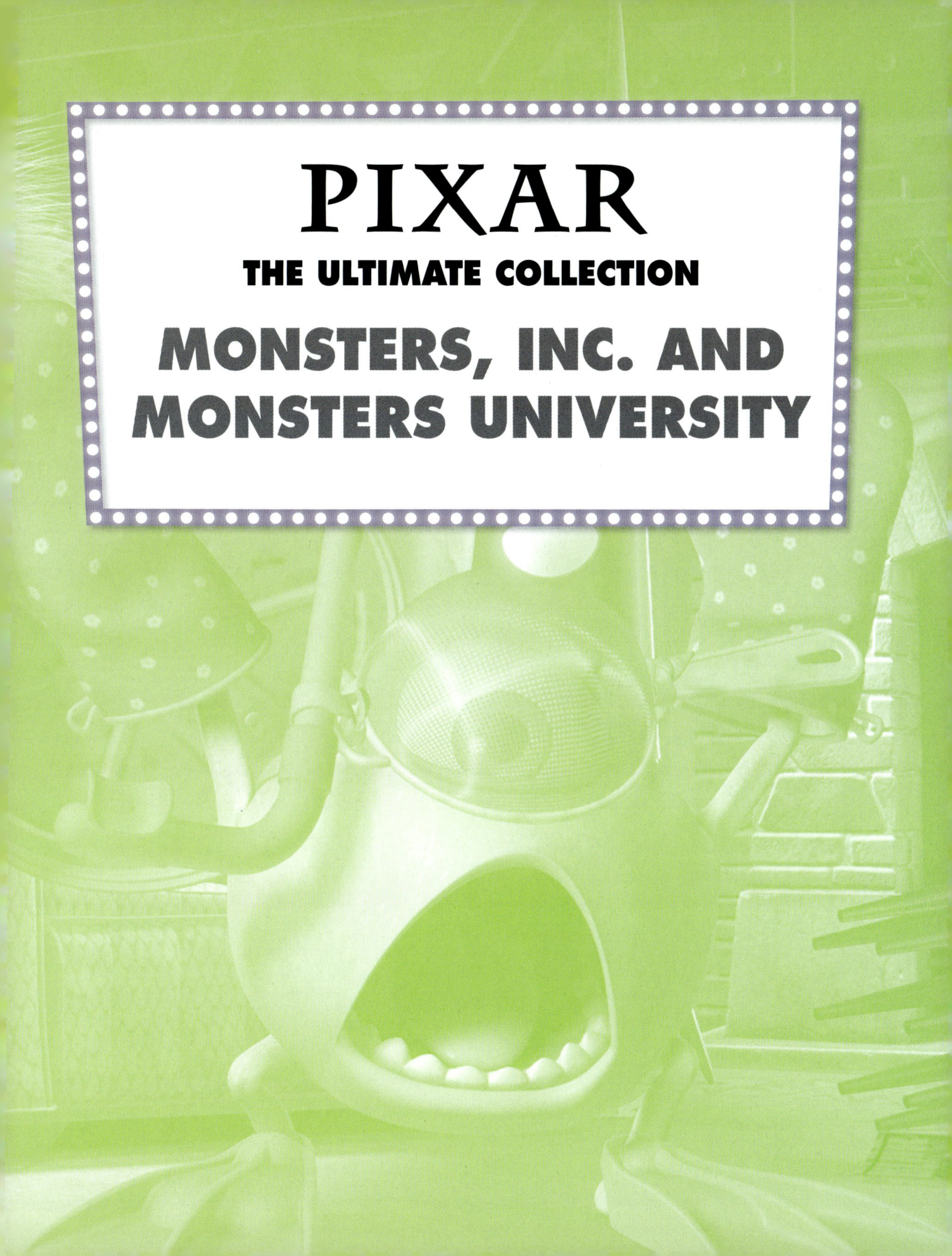

Contents

SULLEY

JAMES P. SULLIVAN, or Sulley, is the top Scarer at Monsters, Inc., a company that provides energy to Monstropolis by capturing the screams of children from the human world. Sulley is fierce on the Scare Floor, but off it, he's as friendly as he is furry.

Dream team
As new Scare Students at Monsters University, it seems that Sulley and Mike are too different to be friends at first. But they soon become extremely close. Now, these best pals live together, work together, and hardly ever argue!

"May the best monster win."

New pal
Monsters believe that human kids are highly dangerous. At first, Sulley is scared of Boo. But he soon grows fond of her and finds a new way to power Monstropolis without scaring anyone – using children's laughter!

Modest monster

Sulley is an A-list celebrity around Monstropolis, but he doesn't let fame go to his furry head. Sulley treats everybody the same, whether they're co-workers or monsters. He's just a regular guy!

MIKE

FAST-LIVING AND FUN-LOVING, Mike is Sulley's Scare Assistant and best pal. He is a real ball of energy. You won't find Mike staying in and watching TV – unless it's to see himself on the new Monsters, Inc. advertisement.

Monster love
Mike and his "Shmoopsie Poo" Celia only have an eye for each other. He treats her to dinner on her birthday and supplies her with an endless stream of compliments, which she loves.

Take the mic, Mike
When Monsters, Inc. changes from scaring kids to making them laugh, Mike puts his comedic skills to the test. Mike even resorts to swallowing his mic to make a child laugh. His jokes definitely need a little more work...

"Nothing is more important than our friendship."

Roar recruit

Mike has plenty of skills to make up for the fact that he looks about as monstrous as a tennis ball. He is a quick learner and can bring out the best in those around him. Once he teams up with Sully at Monsters University, he becomes part of an unstoppable team.

Did You Know?

Mike has always suffered from poor eyesight. He gets his lenses from the upmarket Cyclops Optical. Well, when you've just got one eye, only the best will do!

RANDALL BOGGS

RANDALL BOGGS IS slimy, slippery, and disgusting – and that's just his personality. The meanest monster around, he's Sulley's main rival at Monsters, Inc. Randall is challenging Sulley for the position of top Scarer, but one thing's for sure – he'll never win any popularity prizes!

Secret plan
Randall has created a top secret scream-extracting machine and he plans to test it on a human child. But until he finds one, Mike the monster will have to do!

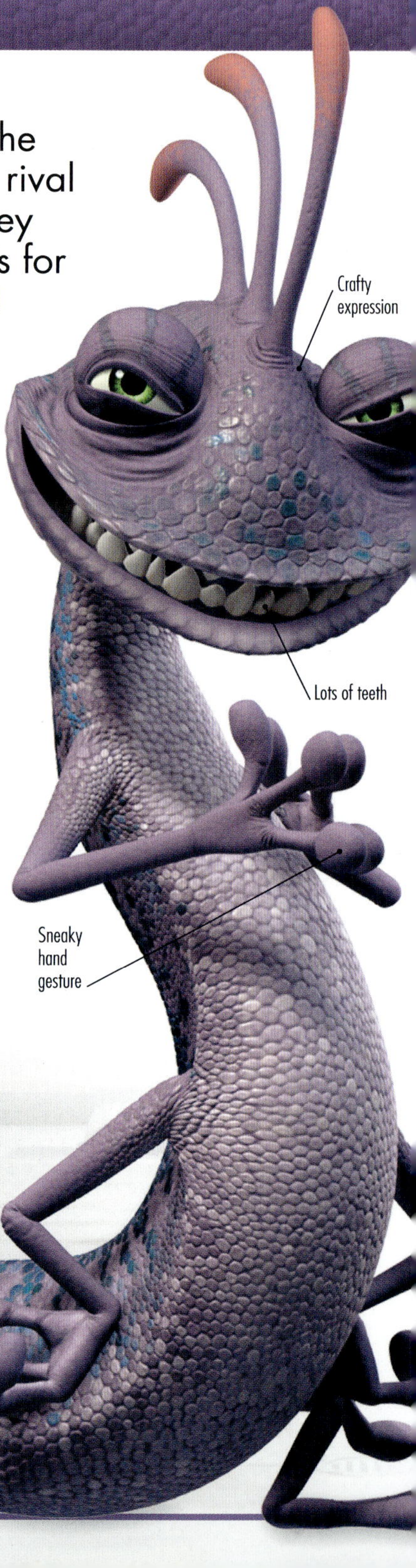

Total transformation
Randall wasn't always a sneaky scarer. When Mike first meets Randy at Monsters University, he is shy, nervous, and sweet-natured. Randy admires his roommate's great determination.

On the prowl

Repugnant Randall is a colour-changing chameleon who can make himself almost invisible. The creep then creeps around scaring children and annoying his rival monsters.

MRS NESBITT

MRS NESBITT IS probably the least scary monster at Monsters, Inc. She runs the Monsters, Inc. school for young monsters with a perfect balance of firmness and understanding. Having four arms means the plump, purple-spotted monster can easily comfort more than one child at a time.

All monsters allowed
Mrs Nesbitt welcomes all monsters in her class. However, she might want to take a closer look at the purple "monster" with the eyes on stalks...

Teacher's pets

All the mini monsters love Mrs Nesbitt. Although they can misbehave sometimes, they think she's a class act and the perfect teacher to keep an eye on them ...although her eyesight might need to be tested!

Did You Know?
Mrs Nesbitt has worked at Monsters, Inc. as a teacher since the company first opened.

CELIA

Did You Know?

The snakes on Celia's head have a mind of their own. They chirp when they are happy and hiss when they are angry!

AS THE RECEPTIONIST at Monsters, Inc., Celia has learned to be super-efficient. She has to greet visitors, answer the phones, and make announcements over the intercom – sometimes all at the same time! It's a pity the five snakes on her head can't help her out.

Mad monster

When Celia and the five snakes on her head get mad, Monstropolis had better watch out! Seeing that her Googly Bear – Mike – and Sulley are trying to escape from Randall, she makes sure she stops the horrible monster from catching them.

"Oh, Googly-woogly, you remembered!"

Concise Celia

Celia has a no-nonsense approach in and out of the office. Although she loves a romantic night out with the apple of her eye, Mike, Celia keeps him on his six toes. If she senses that he is keeping secrets from her, she demands to know the truth – immediately!

True love

Celia and Mike are a match made in monster heaven. Although Mike sometimes makes her mad, she wouldn't change a thing about him.

ROZ

Did You Know?

The CDA saves Monstropolis from human contamination. It works around the clock disinfecting monsters and eliminating human goods.

DISPATCH MANAGER FOR Scare Floor F, Roz is a stickler for the rules. Just one dirty look from this stern-looking giant slug is enough to make all the Scare Assistants tremble with fear, particularly if they haven't handed in their paperwork on time.

Sharp-eyed slug

This sly slug is bossy and conscientious for a reason! As leader of the CDA (Child Detection Agency), she worked undercover at Monsters, Inc. to expose the scandal at the company.

No sweet talking here!

Roz is immune to sweet talk – no matter how hard the assistants try, they just can't shift her permanent frown. There's more to Roz than scowls and sarcasm, however, and she always seems to know exactly what's going on at Monsters, Inc....

"I'm watching you Wazowski, always watching."

BOO

BOO IS ONLY two years old, but she is very brave. The plucky youngster is not afraid to hang out with a bunch of the weirdest-looking oddballs you can find. Boo has a limited vocabulary of about three words, but she has loads of energy and laughs at the most unexpected things, including her monster friends!

No more tears
Boo has a massive effect on Sulley and all of Monstropolis. Thanks to her influence, laughter rather than screams now fuel the city.

Monster disguise
When Boo gets lost in the Monsters, Inc. factory, she tags along with a group of young monsters being shown around the factory. Her monster costume helps her to blend right in.

"Boo!"

Did You Know?
One of Boo's favourite toys is her Yodelling Jessie Cowgirl doll.

Here Kitty, Kitty
Boo is a very curious child and loves to go exploring. This causes some stress for Sulley, her favourite monster and friend. Boo thinks he looks like a giant pussycat and calls him "Kitty".

WATERNOOSE

PROUD, PROPER, AND pretty scary, Henry J. Waternoose is the boss of Monsters, Inc. The company has been in the Waternoose family for three generations, and Henry J. began his illustrious career on the Scare Floor when he was a young monster (a long time ago).

Star pupil
Waternoose is proud of his top Scarer, Sulley, and often uses his super scare skills to show other monsters how it's done.

"I'll kidnap a thousand children before I let this company die!"

Horrible Henry
Waternoose pretends to take care of Boo, but really he is planning to extract screams from her with the horrible scream extracting machine!

Fake friend

Underneath his professional exterior, Waternoose is actually dishonest and devious. He is facing a looming scream shortage and is under intense pressure to get his employees to collect more screams. He will do anything to make his company profitable again, even if it means betraying loyal friends like Sulley.

GEORGE

GEORGE IS ONE of the most laid-back monsters on the Scare Floor. Easygoing and popular, he isn't too bothered about being the best. George would much rather take it easy with the other Scarers and share a joke or two on the Scare Floor than be at the top of the Scarer Leaderboard.

Contamination
Trouble seems to follow poor George everywhere. When a kid's sock gets stuck to his furry back, the CDA is called immediately to catch the contaminated monster. George has a very close shave and loses most of his shaggy fur!

Mild monster

Some might say that George is a little too carefree and, consequently, this accident-prone monster often gets into scrapes. George is good friends with Mike and Sulley, and they often hang out together on the Scare Floor.

Did You Know?
At Monsters University, George was a member of the JOX fraternity. They were the snarliest students on campus!

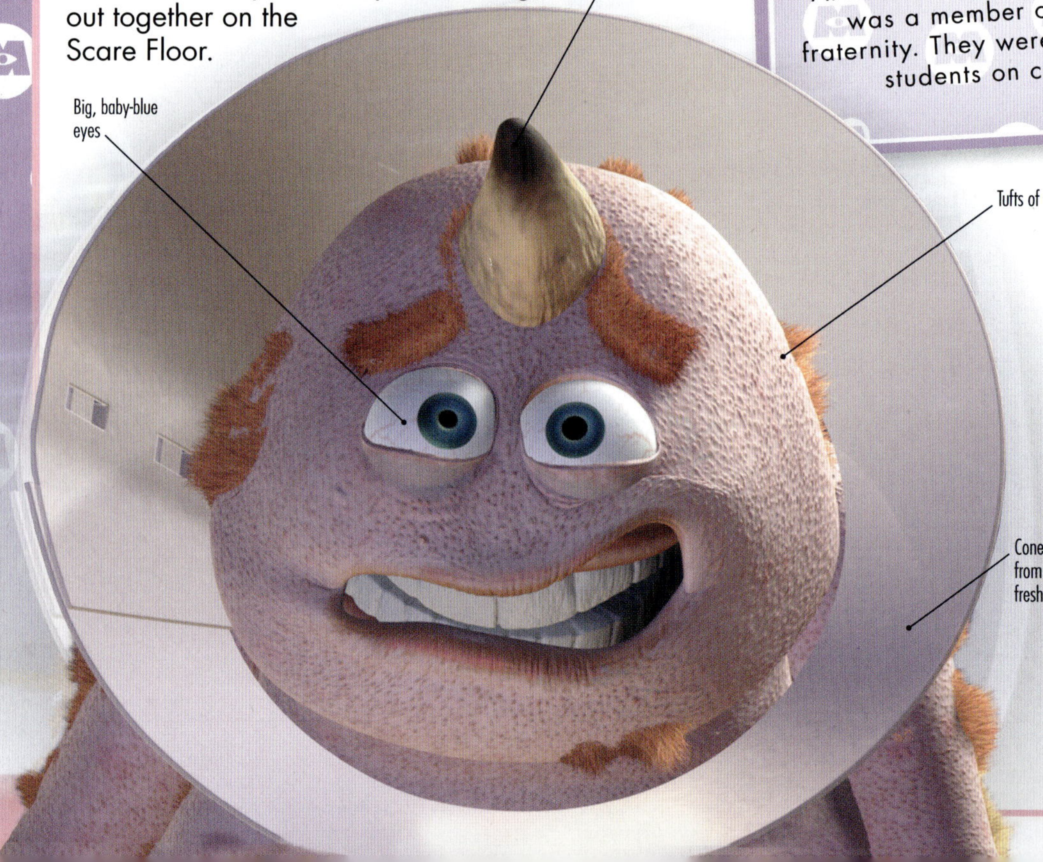

CLAWS

PETE "CLAWS" WARD has the largest, sharpest claws on the Scare Floor, and he's proud of it! Each morning, Claws lovingly extends his talons to their full, terrifying length, ready for a great day of scaring.

Dinnertime
After a hard day's work on the Scare Floor, Claws enjoys nothing more than getting his claws into a bit of sushi at *Harryhausen's* restaurant with his monster pals.

Big softy

Claws isn't actually as fierce as he looks. Nearly being touched by a child can reduce him to a big, blubbering blue mess.

Did You Know?

Claws is close friends with fellow Scarers George and Nick "Lanky" Schmidt.

FUNGUS

GEEKY THREE-EYED Fungus has the terrifying task of being Randall's Assistant. His career may have blossomed with Randall's success, but the experience has made Fungus into a nervous monster. Secretly, he'd rather be inventing crafty contraptions than pandering to the loathsome lizard.

Always on call
Fungus is clever and hardworking – well, he has to be, working for a demanding monster like Randall!

Eyes wide open

Keeping Randall happy can be a terrifying business, and keeping his evil agenda secret is equally scary. Fungus has to keep all three eyes open, just in case something goes wrong.

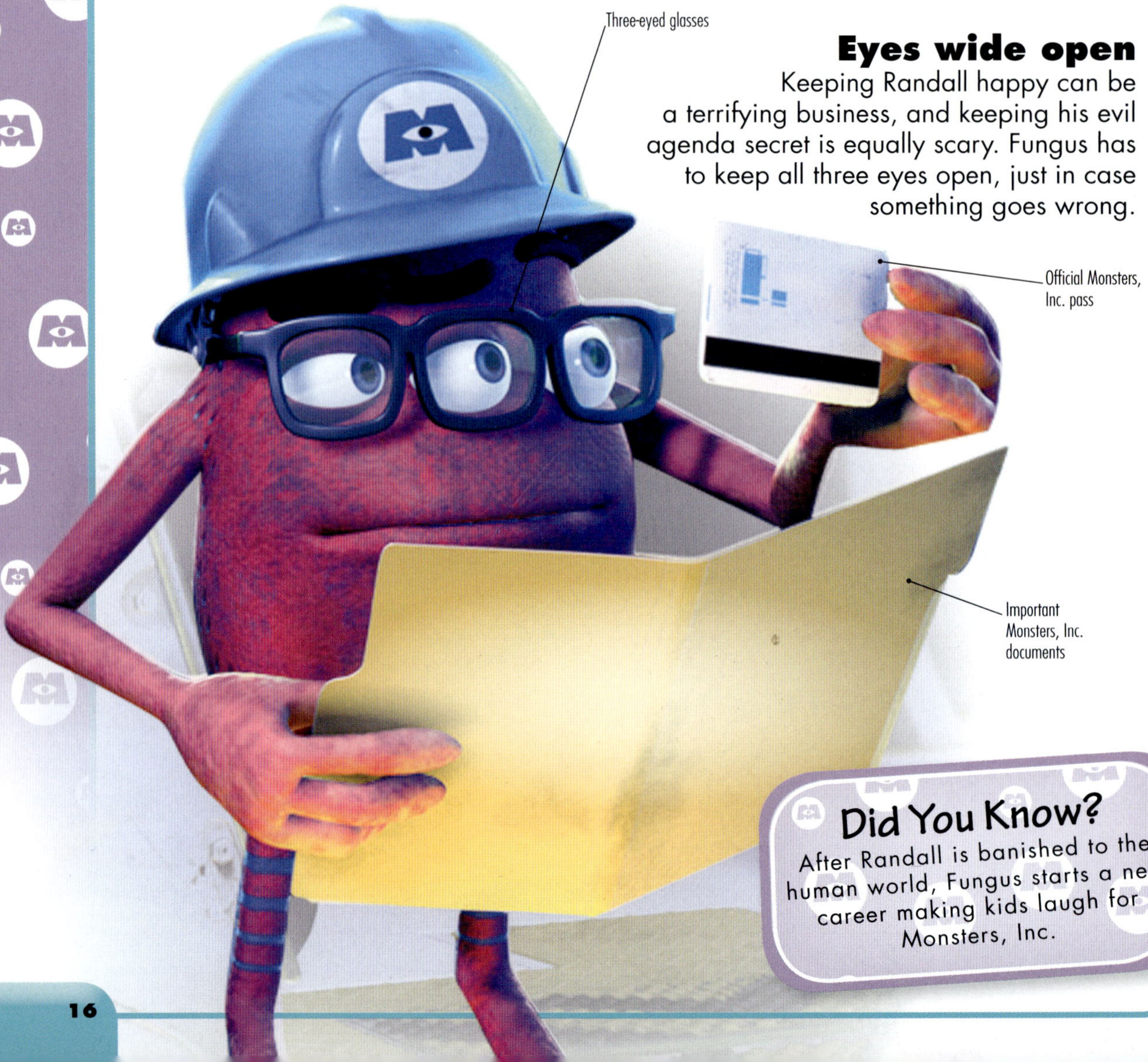

Did You Know?

After Randall is banished to the human world, Fungus starts a new career making kids laugh for Monsters, Inc.

JERRY

AS THE FLOOR manager at Monsters, Inc., Jerry ensures everything runs flawlessly on the Scare Floor. Luckily, Jerry is an organized guy, so panicking monsters, shredded doors, and contamination scares don't fluster him. He works hard to make sure that the maximum amount of screams is captured every day.

Scare challenge
Working on the Scare Floor is a challenge, but this doesn't frighten Jerry – in fact, he relishes his role as manager!

3-2-1-action!
Jerry counts down the seconds left for the monsters to get to work and start scaring.

"We may actually make our quota today!"

Multiskilled

Jerry has learned to deal with all the monstrous egos on the Scare Floor, and he is regarded as a key employee at Monsters, Inc. He even has a speaking part in the firm's TV advertisement.

Did You Know?
Jerry has seven fingers on each hand – handy when he's doing countdowns for the monsters!

NEEDLEMAN

NERDY NEEDLEMAN IS the company caretaker, along with his best pal, Smitty. This odd pair do lots of small but essential jobs, such as pushing carts of scream canisters, operating the door-shredding machine, and straightening out pictures... well, somebody has to!

Did You Know?
Needleman plays Randall Boggs in Mike's play, *Put That Thing Back Where It Came From Or So Help Me.*

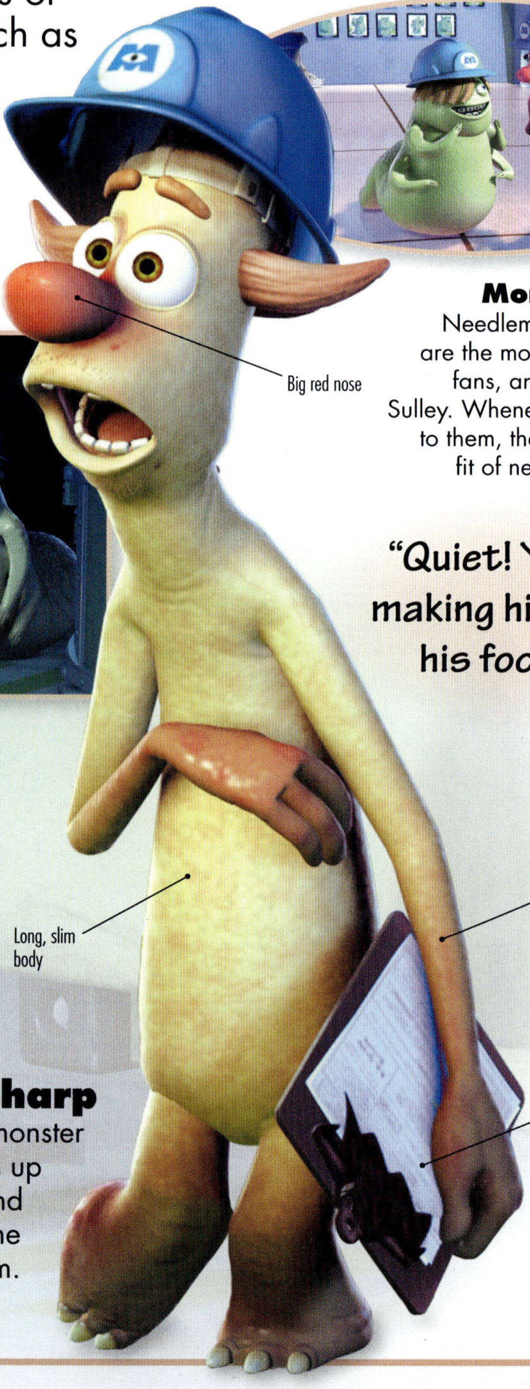

Monster fans

Needleman and Smitty are the monsters' biggest fans, and their hero is Sulley. Whenever he speaks to them, they erupt into a fit of nervous giggles.

"Quiet! You're making him lose his focus."

A dirty job

Needleman and Smitty are a great team. They love their caretaker jobs, even if the work is sometimes dirty – after all, they get to mingle with A-list celebrities like Sulley.

Not so needle sharp

Needleman isn't the sharpest monster in the factory. However, he makes up for this with lots of enthusiasm, and he's a valued member of the Monsters, Inc. team.

SMITTY

WITH HIS BAD HAIRCUT and wonky helmet, Smitty looks awkward and clumsy – and unfortunately his looks don't lie! Together with fellow clumsy caretaker Needleman, the hare brained pair stumble and bumble their way around the factory carrying out various tasks.

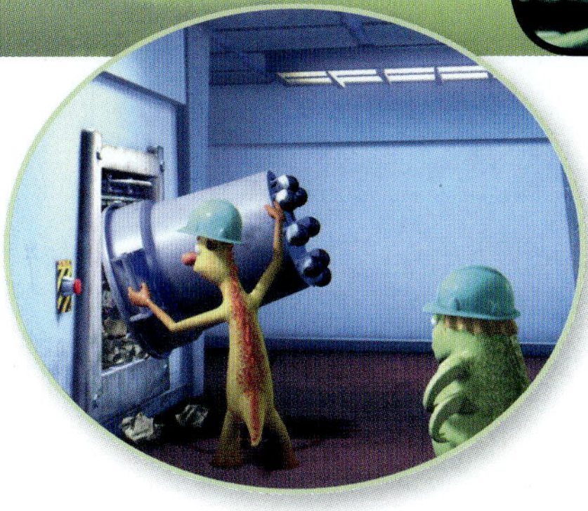

Not on the ball
Needleman and Smitty have short concentration spans and often don't pay attention to the job at hand. They very nearly throw Boo into the rubbish crusher!

Monster hero
It's hard for Smitty to contain his excitement when Sulley says hello to him. He respects the furry monster so much, he insists on calling him Mr Sullivan.

Hard worker

Smitty is smitten with the stars of the Scare Floor, like Sulley – he thinks they are sooo cool. Smitty is a great monster to have around the place – he has a big heart and is always helpful.

Did You Know?
Smitty and Needleman sometimes quarrel. Needleman gets especially annoyed with Smitty when he fails to say Sulley's name correctly!

BILE

THADDEUS BILE, KNOWN as Phlegm to his friends, is a trainee Scarer. He's a popular monster with the other trainees, mainly because he's just as useless as they are! Bile has a lot to learn if he's going to make it onto the payroll...

Fail!

Bile's botched attempt at scaring in the Simulator Room doesn't impress the boss, Waternoose. Going for a "snake-slash-ninja" approach just isn't going to cut it at Monsters, Inc., no matter how much hissing Bile throws in for good measure!

A lot to learn

Bile needs to learn to work on looking terrifying rather than terrified! In the Simulator Room, a robotic child makes the rookie recruit jump so much, Bile ends up in a heap on the floor.

"Uh, my friends call me Phlegm."

CHARLIE

CHARLIE IS GEORGE Sanderson's Assistant on the Scare Floor. With two protruding eyes on stalks, he is great at spying trouble. Unfortunately, Charlie's tentacles are a little trigger-happy – he calls the Child Detection Agency at the slightest sign of a problem.

2319!

Charlie likes to be in the centre of the action at Monsters, Inc. He can often be heard shouting "2319" at the first sign of trouble. This is the code for an emergency, and makes the CDA come running.

Did You Know?
Charlie manages to make it safely back from the Himalayas.

On the ball

Charlie is a very conscientious employee, but this has created problems for his clumsy friend George. Calling in the CDA has resulted in George ending up on crutches with all his fur shaved off!

Banished!

Charlie gets on well with George, and the two firm friends always have fun working in the factory. But George is a little tired of visits from the CDA, and before Charlie can make another call, George pushes him through a door to the Himalayas!

WAXFORD

WAXFORD IS AUGUSTUS "Spike" Jones' Assistant. He is, without a doubt, one of the shiftiest-looking monsters in the factory, but that's because he has five very large eyeballs on stalks. Waxford isn't shifty at all; in fact he is perfectly trustworthy, always keeping an eye – or five – on what's going on.

Did You Know?
Waxford has tentacles instead of feet.

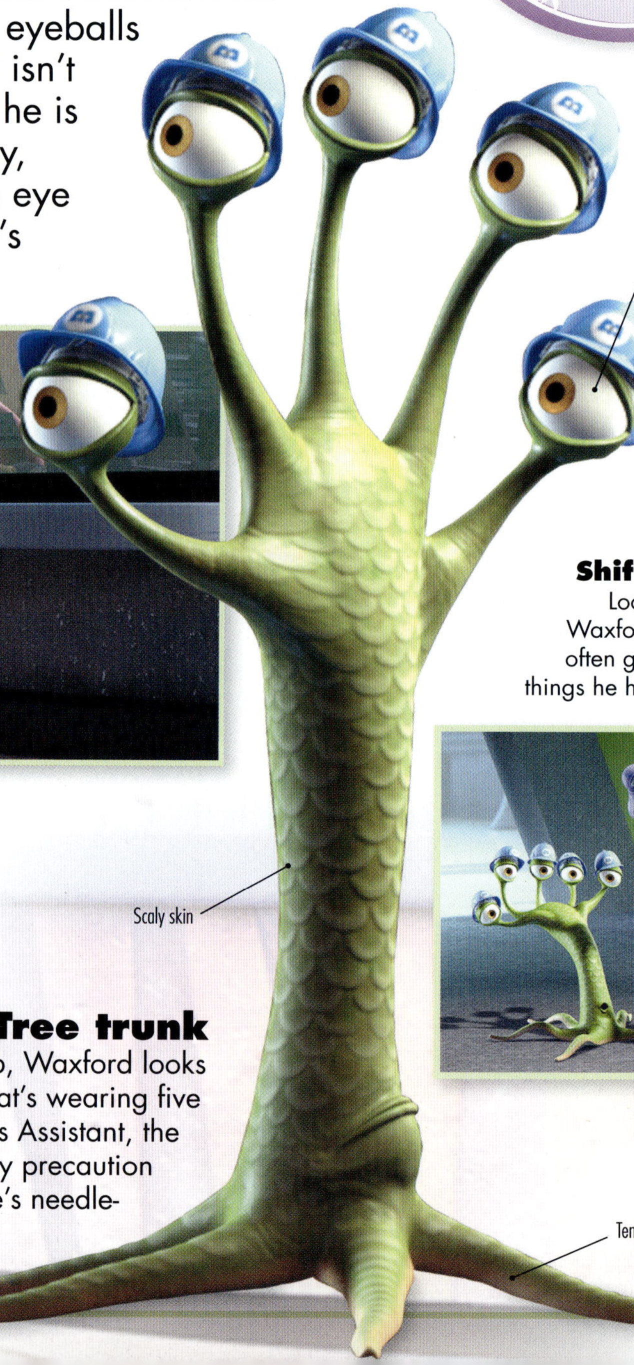

Shift the blame

Looking as shifty as Waxford means that he often gets the blame for things he hasn't even done!

Eye eye

Waxford might have five eyes but he's not as sharp-eyed as Roz. No one is.

Tree trunk

When he's standing up, Waxford looks a little bit like a tree that's wearing five helmets. As Spike's Assistant, the helmets are a necessary precaution to protect him from Spike's needle-sharp spines.

ABOMINABLE SNOWMAN

THE ABOMINABLE SNOWMAN is more amiable than abominable. He's been exiled to the Himalayas for many years, but he isn't complaining. He loves his "winter wonderland", where he can sip a mug of yak's milk in his cozy cave. When Sulley and Mike are banished there by Waternoose, Abominable gives them a warm, Yeti welcome!

Sad Sulley
Despite the Yeti's enthusiastic greeting, Sulley can't help but miss Boo. He comes up with a plan to return to Monstropolis and rescue his favourite youngster.

Sweet treat
Abominable adores lemon-flavoured snowcones and kindly offers the sweet snacks to his guests. However, Mike is more interested in keeping warm!

> "Rule number one out here: always... no, never go out in a blizzard."

Cool guy
The snowman is a friendly giant and always gives travellers a warm welcome in a cold climate. The hospitable Yeti offers shelter from blizzards and an endless supply of lemon-flavoured snowcones.

Did You Know?
Abominable loves his home in the Himalayas so much that he has no plans to return to the human world.

DEAN HARDSCRABBLE

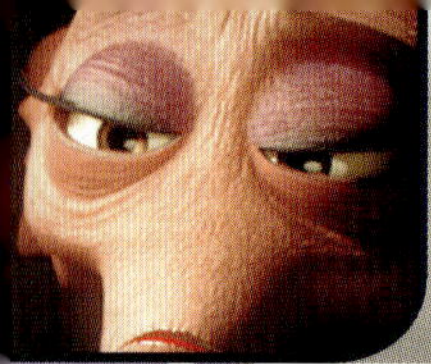

A LIVING LEGEND, this dean casts a long shadow over Monsters University. Dean Hardscrabble believes that monsters exist only to scare, and without that power, they are nobody. Having decided that Mike isn't scary, she considers him finished on the Scaring Programme.

Record holder
The dean's most precious possession is the can that contains her record-breaking scream. This souvenir of her great career is accidentally wrecked by Mike and Sulley.

Games master
When the expelled Mike and Sulley enter the Scare Games, Hardscrabble reluctantly agrees that if their team can win the games, they will be allowed on to the Scaring Programme. Of course, she believes they have no chance!

"Scariness is the true measure of a monster."

Always right
Once this seasoned Scarer has decided that someone isn't scary, she never changes her mind. Being challenged by Mike and Sulley is a whole new experience for her, and one she treats with utter scorn.

Did You Know?
Hardscrabble founded the Scare Games when she was a student, and won four years in a row!

JOHNNY WORTHINGTON

TOP SCARE STUDENT and president of the popular Roar Omega Roar fraternity, Johnny is the monster who seems to have everything. With brains as well as brawn, he rules the roost on campus and decides who is in the "in-crowd" and who gets left behind.

"RORs are the best Scarers on campus."

Team ROR
Johnny and his pals at ROR are all from rich, important families. They are cool, easygoing guys – while everything is going their way. But they turn nasty really fast if someone tries to outdo them.

Big bully
Mike is one of the main victims of Johnny's nasty side. The big college hero just can't stand little guys who don't know their place. He sneeringly calls Mike "Killer" and "beach ball".

Prankster

Sneaky Johnny uses a cruel sense of humour to put his enemies down. When Oozma Kappa impress in the Scare Games, he embarrasses them by tricking them into appearing in a cute photo with glitter confetti, flowers, and stuffed animals!

SQUISHY

CHILDLIKE AND CHEERFUL, this nervous 19-year-old is the heart and soul of the Oozma Kappa gang. Squishy loves to make new members welcome, and if there is anything he can't personally provide, then his mum is happy to step in.

Sulley fan
Squishy is thrilled to have some real scary monsters in the gang – the OKs are sure to do well in the Scare Games with Mike and Sulley on board.

Squishy snaps
Squishy rarely raises his voice, but he does get agitated when his mum is slow to drive off after their trip to Monsters, Inc. Ms Squibbles won't be rushed – she needs to check that all seat-belts have been fastened, and then wants to offer everyone a piece of gum!

"I've never stayed up this late in my life!"

Games hero

Squishy has a gift for fading into the background. It sure comes in handy in the "Avoid the Parent" Scare Games event, when he evades the librarian and takes the flag for his team!

DON CARLTON

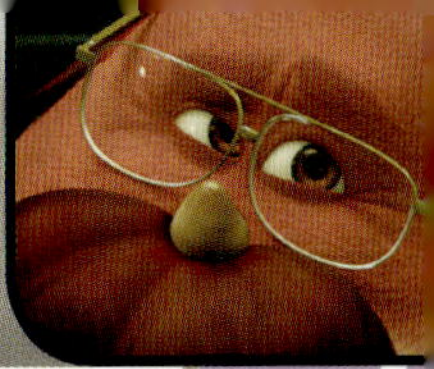

THIS MILD-MANNERED monster is the president of the OKs. Don learned a lot from his early years as a salesman – mainly that he wasn't wanted anymore! Now he has enrolled at MU as a mature student, seeking a new start.

Keep it down!
Deluded Don believed he was the master of the silent scare, until he found out just how noisy his suckers can be. His real talent lies in using them for hanging around in unexpected places!

Top Don
Don's leadership skills shine when the OKs make it to the Scare Games final. He steps out first in the head-to-head against ROR, and earns a high score in the simulator – putting OK in the lead!

Living the dream

Don has a permanently positive outlook on life: when he was let go by his sales company, he refused to throw a pity party and give up! Now he is learning about computers and getting reschooled in Scaring.

Did You Know?

One habit the ex-salesman can't quit is his fondness for handing out business cards. After his successes in the Scare Games, his cards now read "Scarer", rather than "Sales".

TERRI AND TERRY

THEY SAY THAT two heads are better than one, but this split personality isn't always so sure! One thing the Oozma Kappa brothers Terri and Terry Perry do share is a love of bickering – and a dream of becoming Scarers.

Party monsters
Terri and Terry have a gift for crazy dance routines, but can't always agree on when or where to perform them. The failed routine usually ends with an argument and public humiliation.

Disco ball drop
Terri and Terry plan a disco ball welcome party for new members Mike and Sulley. When it crashes straight to the floor, they confess they've never had a real party!

"You should wake up embarrassed!"

Double trouble

Despite being physically inseparable, these brothers have very different personalities. "Terry with a 'y'" is older by several seconds, and sees himself as the wise, old cynic of the duo. "Terri with an 'i'" is the naïve youngster who often gets put in his place. But they can work together; their misdirection skills help the OKs confuse the librarian in the second Scare Games challenge.

ART

A creature of mystery, this new age philosophy student is a loyal member of Oozma Kappa. In a time of crisis, he can always be relied upon – to do something unexpected and bizarre!

Meditation guru
Art is scared of working-out because he claims he is frightened of getting too big. He prefers meditation and yoga to exercise – as long as he can do it in his own unique way.

Dream keeper
Art keeps a dream journal. It's a kooky habit he thinks everyone should practise—he even gives Mike and Sulley their own books to do it in.

Confession!
When nearly caught on the roof of Monsters, Inc., Art shocks his pals by confessing that he was once in prison!

Did You Know?
Art has a weird curiosity about everything – including touching the highly toxic glow urchins he was told to avoid in the first Scare Games event!

Mystery monster

Prone to dropping baffling remarks about his past and hobbies, Art claims to have an extra toe (not that you can see it). He is also fond of sewer 14, which he says is his favourite of all the sewers on campus.

DK Penguin Random House

Editors Vicky Armstrong, Ellie Barton, Jo Casey, Beth Davies, Helen Murray
Designers Richard Horsford, Poppy Joslin, David McDonald, Mark Penfound, Satvir Sihota, Lisa Sodeau, Rhys Thomas
Senior Production Editor Jennifer Murray
Senior Production Controller Mary Slater
Publishing Operations Executive Becca Pitt
Managing Editors Pete Jorgensen, Paula Regan
Managing Art Editor Jo Connor
Publishing Director Mark Searle

Written by Steve Bynghall, Jo Casey, Glenn Dakin, Clare Hibbert, Julia March, Helen Murray, and Catherine Saunders

Acknowledgements: The publisher would like to thank Kayla Dugger at DK, and Chelsea Alon, Chuck Wilson, Scott Tilley, and Tony Fejeran at Disney Publishing.

This edition published in 2021
First published in Great Britain in 2020 by
Dorling Kindersley Limited
One Embassy Gardens, 8 Viaduct Gardens, London SW11 7BW
A Penguin Random House Company

002-323814-Sept/2020

Contains content previously published in *Disney Pixar Character Encyclopedia* (2019)

The authorised representative in the EEA is Dorling Kindersley Verlag GmbH, Arnulfstr. 124, 80636 Munich, Germany.

A CIP catalogue record for this book is available from the British Library.

ISBN 978-0-24148-816-4

Printed and bound in China

For the curious

www.dk.com
www.disney.com

MIX
Paper from responsible sources
FSC www.fsc.org FSC™ C018179

This book was made with Forest Stewardship Council ™ certified paper – one small step in DK's commitment to a sustainable future. For more information go to www.dk.com/our-green-pledge